Hiking ❶ Walking ❶ Bicycling ❶ guide

KATY
TRAIL

Jefferson City to Boonville
plus a side trip to Arrow Rock

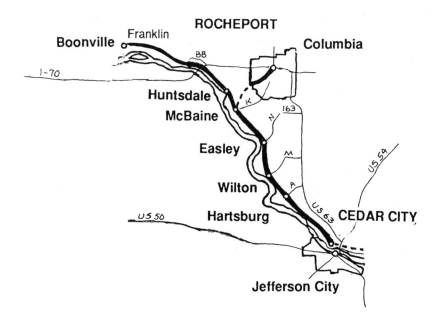

Sally Winters & Sharon Kinney Hanson

Acknowledgments

Sally and Sharon wish to thank the following people who have helped make this guidebook happen: Monett Lite (Friends of Rocheport Museum); Pat Jackson (Boonville Chamber of Commerce); Kathy Borgman (Executive Director, Friends of Arrow Rock); Gene Owens (South Howard County Historical Society); Randal Clark, Darwin Hindman, David Sapp; the Cole County Historical Society--Gloria Overfelt, Janis Lauer, Elizabeth Rozier; Department of Natural Resources staff, especially Ken Oidtman, Debbie Schnack, Richard Forry, Bill Palmer; Dave Rechtien (Easley General Store Manager); Steve Kappler (MO Division of Tourism); Department of Conservation, especially Kathy Love and Bernadette Dryden; Dale Renkemeyer (Mid-Missouri Computer Services); Madeline Matson, Stonge, Richard, and various friends and pets for listening, encouraging, and believing.

CONTENTS

Photo courtesy Nick "Danger" Decker, DNR

This book is dedicated to

...my unbridled Bruiser, lifelong companion
  whose spirit I know
  sniffs the trail still. (SKH)

...my parents, J. Warren and Kitty Getz, for
  stimulating my interest in nature,
  history, and travel. (SW)

Preface

The story of the KATY Trail began in 1986 when flood damages and economics forced the Missouri-Kansas-Texas Railroad to abandon its 199.9 miles from Machens (near the Missouri/Mississippi confluence, 20 miles northeast of St. Charles) to Sedalia, Missouri. KATY Trail owes its existence to the private sector, government, grass roots groups, and private philanthropy -- to people who wanted to protect this corridor of beautiful land that holds much historic significance. They prevented the countryside from being cut up into pieces for sale or default to the trail's adjoining landowners and others.

Fortunately, the U.S. Congress passed Section 8(d) of the National Trails Systems Act, giving states a means of acquiring right-of-ways for trail use. The Interstate Commerce Commission certified the KATY corridor for trail use in lieu of abandonment providing that the state develop and maintain it, and ICC permits the return of the corridor to railroad use if public necessity requires it.

The state and railroad officials agreed on a fair price but when some sectors of the public realized the trail's potential, opposing opinions arose. Many saw value in its economic, recreational and education benefits.

Trail supporters (conservationists, recreationists, chambers of commerce, historic and health groups) organized -- using the name Katy Trail Coalition (which I was privileged to chair). WIth thousands of signatures to present to the governor, KTC members lobbied, testified at hearings, debated, published newsletters, and rallied actively for the trail for five years. When the trail-cause caught Edward D. Jones' attention, Missouri's legislators were embroiled with controversy. Owner of a large stock brokerage firm, Jones worked with trail supporters "in the trenches" and then contributed $200,000 to the estate to buy the railroad's interest. His unprecedented philanthropy was inspirational. He later gave two million dollars for surfacing the trail, assuring that the trail would "happen."

When in 1987, the governor authorized the state to apply to the ICC for trail use, opponents filed suit. After about four years, the U.S. Supreme Court settled the matter. The state went forward with construction, using Jones' money, and avoided legislative appropriation delays. The first segment of KATY opened April 1989.

The extensive publicity generating from struggles to make KATY Trail happen created heavy use from the first day the trail opened to the public. Users are enjoying the benefits of exercise and beautiful surroundings, but they were missing much of interest because they had little information about what is there, along the trail.

This book provides users the opportunity to enjoy much of the trail's cultural and natural history. People select their favorite part of the trail; many agree that the guide *KATY Trail: Jefferson City to Boonville* covers the most interesting and beautiful stretch of the whole trail.

This guide helps users to see and do more, thus have more fun along the trail. It recalls cultural and natural history along Missouri's major rail route. Persons using this guide find themselves communicating with history by being on the very spot that an event occurred . . . maybe it's an event the reader just learned about, a place that Lewis and Clark camped and described, for example.

The KATY Trail offers fascinating geology, and this guide helps the user to see and appreciate it.

Getting lost on the trail can't happen; after all, it's about ten feet wide and lies on an identifiable gravel-graded railroad. But sometimes a user wonders "how far it is to the next trail head?" or "just where am I relative to other things I'm interested in?" The guide's maps detail and identify places relative to trail mile post markers; they make using the trail interesting and fun, as do the many photographs and illustrations.

Writers of *KATY Trail* described features of interest in the towns adjoining the trail; their list of seasonal events along the trail, tempt readers to expand their horizons by getting off the trail for a while to see or participate in them . . . to so a little shopping, stop for a refreshment or meal. Why be in a hurry?

Knowing that people will come from long distances to enjoy KATY Trail, and wanting users to enjoy themselves by being properly equipped, the authors included such useful information as equipment tips, weather information, and reminders on good trail user conduct.

I am delighted to see the *KATY Trail: Jefferson City to Boonville* published. It is easy to read and designed to make a trail user's experience satisfying. I think it will succeed.

Darwin A. Hindman, Jr.

Guide Overview

In our 50-mile trek starting from the river bottoms at Jefferson City, striding westward as did Lewis and Clark, we pick up bits of history and culture, flavors of local grub and lodging, and, along the pathway, perhaps make new friends---two legged, four legged, and, some, legless. Passing through the towns of the KATY Trail, we catch echoes of Missouri's voices---Daniel Boone, Kit Carson, Sacajawea, Tom Jefferson, Lewis and Clark, Hannah Cole, Quantrill, Kimzey. Events we only read about in history books --The Louisiana Purchase, Manifest Destiny, Missouri Compromise, Santa Fe Trail---come to life on Missouri's KATY Trail.

Highway signs mark the 1804 Lewis and Clark route.

Along the Missouri River bluffs, through the corridor of occasional foothills, KATY Trail may reach in a few years, somewhat horizontally, 200 miles across the state's midsection. Beneath the trail's flat hard-packed chat surface runs the abandoned railbed of the once-almighty Missouri-Kansas-Texas Railroad. People called it The MKT, this rail that followed along the banks of the shifting path of the Missouri River. Now, the KATY Trail invites people who love to walk, bicycle, hike.

This guide provides a look at some (not all) historic and natural sites along the KATY, and gives useful information about lodging and repasts as well as other necessities.

KATY Trail opened for public use in April 1990, a product of the U.S. National Trail Systems Act which allows conversion of abandoned railroad lines into recreational trails as a means to maintain the right-of-way for possible future use as a rail road. Upon its completion, KATY Trail may

DNR's notice to KATY-users.

Notice KATY-wampus lay-out, here and elsewhere.

extend from St. Louis to Kansas City via a Rock Island line which crosses the KATY at Windsor, 15 miles southwest from Sedalia. It is managed by the Missouri Department of Natural Resources.

KATY Trail offers much to many year round. With few and very slight inclines, this flat railcar-wide trail allows easy travel by skinny tire or mountain bicycles, and wheelchairs. People stroll the trail short distances, enjoying Mother Nature's beautiful sights. Some travel long routes, for adventures of varying pace and length. Hikers of the 1990 cross country HikaNation (which promoted a 5000 mile transcontinental hiking and biking path, the American Discovery Trail) used this central Missouri section of the trail. As trees begin to leaf in the spring, KATY Trail displays a myriad of greens, from delicate lime shades to dark, alluring moss greens. Red bud, dogwood, and the shag "present" early with blossoms. The dogwood, the state tree, is in bloom by the month of May. In the fall, oak trees turn into a range of browns and golds; a variety of maple trees riot in spectacular reds and oranges. This area becomes lush with wildflowers: black-eyed susans, pussy's toes, Rue, spiderwort, violet, May apple, Queen Anne's lace, yarrow, ox-eyed daisy, sunflower, goldenrod, wild sweet William (flock) and blue-eyed Mary. Much of the trail is also lined with giant ragweed, which aggravates from August until a killing frost, which may not occur until November. Allergy sufferers, beware! And because this section of KATY exists in a Missouri River flood plain, parts of the trail may be temporarily washed out during our rainy seasons, early spring and late fall.

This guide to KATY Trail covers 50 miles of the trail from Jefferson City through Boonville, with a side trip into Arrow Rock and Boone's Lick State Historic Site. Although much of this section of the trail parallels the

Missouri River, at times it also goes through private farmland (Posted: No trespassing) and at other times through forests and near river bottom lands. The forests contain silver maple, American elm, black walnut, green ash, burr oak, and sycamore, and provide cover to many varieties of wildlife.

KATY Trail also eases "KATY Trail-ers" (walkers, hikers, cyclists) through two wildlife areas administerd by Missouri's Department of Conservation: Eagle Bluffs Wildlife Area (wetlands south of McBaine) and Davisdale Wildlife Area (south of New Franklin). Historically, most of central Missouri is called Boonslick Country; the term usually refers to this section of the trail's most western part.

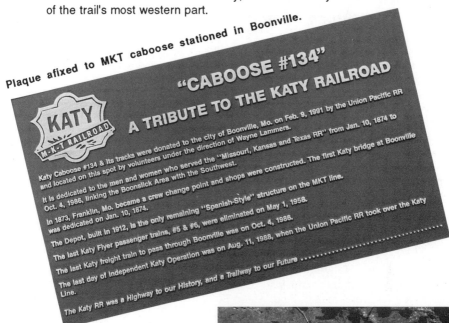

Plaque afixed to MKT caboose stationed in Boonville.

"CABOOSE #134"
A TRIBUTE TO THE KATY RAILROAD

Katy Caboose #134 & its tracks were donated to the city of Boonville, Mo. on Feb. 9, 1991 by the Union Pacific RR and located on this spot by volunteers under the direction of Wayne Lammers.

It is dedicated to the men and women who served the "Missouri, Kansas and Texas RR" from Jan. 10, 1874 to Oct. 4, 1986, linking the Boonslick Area with the Southwest.

In 1873, Franklin, Mo. became a crew change point and shops were constructed. The first Katy bridge at Boonville was dedicated on Jan. 10, 1874.

The Depot, built in 1912, is the only remaining "Spanish-Style" structure on the MKT line.

The last Katy Flyer passenger trains, #5 & #6, were eliminated on May 1, 1958.

The last Katy freight train to pass through Boonville was on Oct. 4, 1986.

The last day of independent Katy Operation was on Aug. 11, 1988, when the Union Pacific RR took over the Katy Line.

The Katy RR was a Highway to our History, and a Trailway to our Future ....

Sculptured MKT logo, on the bluffs along the Trail.

It's a legend...It illustrates the truth.
It does not tell it ···

William Trevor, 1986
News From Ireland

River & Railroad History

Missouri has been called The Mother of the West because (among other reasons) the state's second longest waterway---the Missouri River---provided significant access to The West. Organized as a territory in 1812, Missouri became the 24th state admitted to the Union in 1821.

American Indian culture in Missouri's mid-section (where Katy trail exists) dates from the Woodland Period (1000BC - 900AD). Graham Cave (54 miles east of Rocheport on I-70) is a remnant of a culture existing 10,000 years ago that lasted until about 1000 years ago.

Prior to the 1803 Louisiana Purchase, Missouri Territory was the home of many native tribes, among them the Osage, Kickapoo, Sioux, Cherokee, and the Missouris. By way of treaty, Osage Indians were moved from the mouth of the Osage River (southeast of Jefferson City) to Saline County (northeast of Kansas City). The Missouris, the Sac, the Fox tribes lived north of the Missouri River. Eventually they were altogether pushed off their homeland and out of Missouri Territory.

These Native peoples maintained agricultural and hunting economies; evidence found near Lamine, at the mouth of the Missouri, reveals that they smelted lead, about 5000 pounds of it in a summer's season. They gardened, gathered wild food, fished, hunted. The Missouris wore copper, brass, and beaded jewelry, and like the Osage, traded these and other goods with European explorers and settlers. In 1803, President Thomas Jefferson promoted the purchase of the Louisiana Territory from the French, who had claimed this land from Spanish rule. At the time of this purchase, 10,000 settlers had moved into Missouri, including 1,500 Black Americans.

Once the vast Louisiana Territory came under the dominion of the American government, Jefferson commissioned Meriwether Lewis (who engaged William Clark) to explore northwesterly along the Missouri River and to determine a route to the Pacific Ocean by crossing through this important land acquisition. Lewis and Clark set out in three boats (much like Christopher Columbus did) on May 14, 1804 from DuBois (now the Wood River) near St Louis. Forty-three men composed this Corps of Discovery Expedition, traveling four or five miles on some days, and on other days venturing 26 to 27 miles. Though both Lewis and Clark documented their expedition in diaries, it was naturalist William Clark who spent much time walking the shores of the river, noting aspects of natural history. Lewis' journal shows entries of the number of mosquitoes, flies, ticks, and chiggers. Camping along the Moreau Creek near Jefferson City, one member of the Discovery Corps, Sargent Charles Floyd, described the Jefferson City area as:

"butifull (sic) a peas (sic) of land as I ever saw."

Also noted were the number of (now extinct) green paroquets [also parroquets] in the area, and descriptions of limestone bluffs. On June 6, they camped near (Daniel) Boone's Cave; June 7, Clark explored an area near Rocheport, noting numerous rattlesnakes as well as Native American pictographs; on June 9 they passed Arrow Rock. Most of these pictographs, unfortunately, were destroyed as the Missouri-Kansas-Texas Railroad lines were being laid.

Once the natives were "being resettled," the towns of Franklin and Boonville thrived. By 1820, Howard and Cooper counties amassed 20,000 homesteaders, approximately one-third the population of the territory known as Missouri. Sometime after statehood, a Missouri law prohibited Native Americans from living in the state from 1834 to 1909.

Expansionists and settlers used the Missouri River as an access to explore the countryside. An early explorer, a Frenchman, Etienne de Bourgmont, traveled the Missouri River in 1714 to the Platte River, and trudged upward to South Dakota. The 1795 Spanish Treaty encouraged settlers to establish themselves in Missouri, and by the end of the War of 1812, when hostilities between settlers and remaining tribes were diminishing, more and more Westward-Ho-ers came via wagons and steamboats to Missouri.

Trail pastoral,   north of Easley.

The Missouri River and the state of Missouri are namesakes of the Native American tribe, the Missouris (a fact often overlooked). Regardless of how you hear it pronounced (Mizzurah or Mizzuree) the word, translated into English, conveys reference to Native Americans who first inhabited and revered this land: they were "people of the big canoes." McClure's *History of Missouri* (published some 10 years after Native Americans regained the right to live in Missouri), claims that indian agent William Clark observed the surrender of indian titles to Missouri soil, in 1832. McClure "credits" Clark with making the 1836 treaty with indians for the Platte Purchase, which moved the Missouris away from the Missouri River.

More recently, Missouri native troubadour Bob Dyer of Boonville fame composed and recorded in 1983 many of his folk tunes ("River of the Big Canoes," "Ballad of Boone's Lick," etc.). They're catchy, easy to sing, and in singing them, one finds that they hold trace history of Missouri and the Missouri River, as do all of Dyer's originals. Dyer's song book, and music (his voice, his instrumentation) on audio tapes and compact disc are available: Songteller Bob Dyer, 513 High St., Boonville, 65233.

With its easterly port stretching from the confluence of the Mississippi River in St. Louis, porting in Kansas City, and winding to St. Joseph and beyond, the Missouri River charts-in as the state's 2nd longest river. Jacques Marquette (a priest) and Sieur Joliet in their 1673 explorations called this body of water the River Pekistanoui, using the Illini tribe word meaning "muddy water." According to *Missouri: Its People and Its Progress*, the French explorer La Salle never set foot on Missouri soil nor touched toe into its main river. However, La Salle claimed all the land west of the Mississippi River, naming it the Louisiana Territory, in honor of his King Louis XIV. Previously Spain   governed as well as it could the vastness of that area.

This may be more history than you need or want to know. However, if you're "settled in," so to speak, for a moment of rest from walking or bicycling the trail, perhaps you've girded understanding from this read about the ethnically-mixed flavor of Missouri river/trail towns you'll encounter along your way. On the other hand, if you're a history buff...

Over time, the Big Muddy Missouri River earned the appelation of "Old Misery." In a somewhat romantic vein, Albert Richardson (pre-Civil War *New York Tribune* reporter) noted the uninviting nature of this forceful stream and commented on its dark beauty at dawn and at sunset while proclaiming it magnificent at moonlight.

According to Thomas Hart Benton (a Missouri man of color): "The Missouri River is a little too thick to swim in and not quite thick enough to walk on."

The banks of the Missouri River mainly are of a soil that lends itself to erosion, a soil prime for sandbar creations. Trees, grappling for growth along the river's shores, slipped easily into the river and compounded into sizeable snags, becoming serious hazards for river traffic. The Missouri's current shifted frequently and at times its main channel shifted dramatically, adjusting the history of some towns trying to establish themselves along shorelines. One passenger on the *John Golong* steamboat during the gold

River of the Big Canoes

Words and Music by Bob Dyer

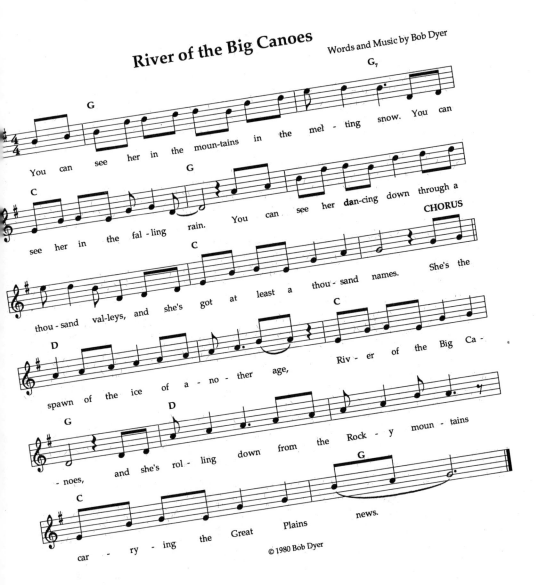

You can see her in the moun-tains in the mel-ting snow. You can see her in the fal-ling rain. You can see her dan-cing down through a thou-sand val-leys, and she's got at least a thou-sand names. She's the spawn of the ice of a-no-ther age, Riv-er of the Big Ca-noes, and she's rol-ling down from the Rock-y moun-tains car-ry-ing the Great Plains news.

CHORUS

© 1980 Bob Dyer

River of the Big Canoes

You can see her in the mountains in the melting snow.
You can see her in the falling rain.
You can see her dancing down through a thousand valleys,
And she's got at least a thousand names.

> She's the spawn of the ice of another age,
> River of the Big Canoes,
> And she's rolling down from the Rocky Mountains
> Carrying the Great Plains news.

Down the Yellowstone and the Musselshell,
Down the Milk and the Little Mo,
Down the James and the Grand and the White and the Bad,
The Cheyenne and the wild Moreau.

When the Frenchmen found her she was Pekitanoui,
A muddy river wild and free,
And they gave her the name of the Indians who lived there,
The people called the Missouri [Mizz-ou-ree].

She's been a river of fur and a river of gold,
A river of crazy schemes.
She's been a steamboat wrecker and a river of coal,
A river of broken dreams.

She's a ghost in the night when the moon is full,
A spirit in the mist at dawn.
She's the light in the eye of a painter's mind,
The music in a poet's song.

River of the Big Canoes

Ballads from the Heartland
Bob Dyer

Treasure in the River

Bob Dyer

rush days noted that snags everywhere made river travel perilous. Consequently, a variety of boats were tried and tested on the Missouri River, as they transported both people and merchandise. French explorers navigated 20-30 foot log canoes called pirouges, generally made from cottonwood trees, which are still plentiful in Missouri. These magnificent trees grow abundant along the trail around the picturesque little town of Easley.

Missouri claims the famous Dan'l Boone as her own, regardless of the fact that Boone was born in Pennsylvania (the same year as George Washington). Daniel Boone arrived in Missouri circa 1798. Boone's Lick Trail (or Trace) was the first land route west of St. Louis, and it was a route traveled by Boone's sons, who horsed, horse 'n buggied, or wagoned their way from their home in St. Charles County to the saline springs. A stage coach rattled back and forth on Boone's Lick Trail by 1820.

Manuel Lisa, an early Spanish fur trader, navigated keelboats up the Missouri as early as 1807. Perceiving fur trading as a way to open-up the west, Señior Lisa tried to create peaceful relationships with Native Americans. Lisa's wife (whose name, like those of so many women, isn't given in texts) was reported to be the first white woman to ascend the Missouri. Lisa made 12 to 13 trips each year, but when he died in 1820, much of his "peaceful" sentiment died with him. Another woman of courage, Sacajawea (AKA Bird Woman) and her child (also nameless in texts) joined Lewis and Clark when they reached the Kansas City area, April 7, 1805.

Keelboats eventually carried 15-30 tons of goods essential to frontier life. Ferry trade flourished across the Missouri; the town of Rocheport had its first ferry in 1819. But steamboats soon became the major means of transportation. The SS Independence ported herself in Franklin and Boonville in 1819, the first to arrive in central Missouri.

Far and wide, the Missouri River was considered as the most treacherous body of water in Louisiana Territory, so much so that riverboat captains established reputations for themselves as they developed navigating skills in this snag-infested river. Skillful captains often earned over $1000 per month. Many steamboats met their makers (so to speak), wrecking on snags or sandbars; some sank, forever unretrievable, to swift-swirling muddy bottoms. Robert Fulton's steamboat design proved inadequate for the Mighty Missouri. (Fulton's namesake, the town of Fulton, is about 23 miles north of the trail from Jefferson City.) Captain Henry Shreve redesigned Fulton's engine for Missouri River navigation and he invented a snag-boat to overcome the hazards of travel on the Missouri. Soon "spoonbill" bows allowed steamers to glide over shallow areas, and "riggings" on front masts allowed boats to be raised-off sandbars; by "grasshoppering," they avoided these sand blockades. Evenso, a steamboat's life expectancy on the Missouri River was a slight three years, somewhat less than on lesser rivers. However, "a boat with a good freight trip could pay for itself in one trip, and certainly in a single season," according to James Swift, Steamboating and Trans-shipment on the Missouri River.

The American sycamore (a snagger of giant proportions).

The Arabia Riverboat Museum, in Kansas City, displays cargo from the S.S. Arabia which in 1856 was swallowed by the Missouri near Kansas City. Recently exhumed, cargo consisted of hardware, dry goods,

"perfume from France, trade beads from eastern Europe, rifles from Belgium, dishware from England, tobacco from Latin America, silk from China."

Thus, European and Far East exotica floated into America's heartland.

When the Missouri-Kansas-Texas Railroad busted across the prairie, the era of iron rails dawned.

KATY TRAIL 20

A Geologist's Look at the Trail

KATY Trail passes through what geologists divide into three natural regions: Missouri Rhineland, White Cliff, and the Boone's Lick Regions.

The Missouri Rhineland begins at the bluffs from Jefferson City north to about a mile south of Wilton. Formed during the Ordovician period (430 million years ago), the rock is light brown to gray and consists of dolomite, chert, and quartz sandstone.

Not of Dover, but north to Rocheport are the White Cliffs of...tall Burlington limestone. These cliffs (or bluffs) contain the remains of crinoids, also called "sea lilies." The White Cliffs of Rocheport were formed during the Pennsylvania era (225 million years ago) when the land there was covered with seas.

The Boone's Lick Region, north of Rocheport, is characterized by limestone bluffs of less stature and with a number of salt springs or salt licks. These limestone bluffs with top layer of clay were formed during the Mississippian era (350 years ago).

Most of this area is glaciated plains, the land flattened by glaciers, with erosion beginning 10,000 BC. Limestone formed from the marine life that existed when seas covered Missouri 250 to 500 million years ago. Missouri's caves along KATY Trail were formed by erosion caused by water running beneath the limestone.

Almost sunset, along the Trail near Providence.

There is about the Missouri landscape something intimate and known to me...I seem to know what is going to be there, what the creek beds and the sycamore and walnuts lining them will look like, and what the color of the bluffs will be.
--Thomas Hart Benton, 1937

Jefferson City's 2nd capitol building and c. 1842 Lohman's Landing.
Cole County Historical Museum photo.

Jefferson City (MP 143.2) - Population 35,481 Elevation 420' at trailhead - Cole & Callaway Counties

The 50 mile Jefferson City-Boonville Section of the KATY Trail begins in the river bottoms, in North Jefferson City, near the northern flank of the Jefferson City bridge over the Missouri River. This area, annexed by the City of Jefferson in the last few years, is known as Cedar City. Laid out c. 1870, Cedar City got its name from its profusion of "bluff dwelling" cedars. A few wild goats still graze on (and grace) one of the last (and largest) bluffs west of Highway 63. Some say only the pure of heart see "Missouri's flyin'wild Billy-gruff goats" but we've seen 'em; maybe you will too as you pause at Mile Post 145.5 to look for them.

At this point on KATY Trail, you're in Callaway County, which is named after the grandson of Daniel Boone, Captain James Callaway. Capt. Callaway met his maker during an "Indian frickass" in the first decade of the 19th Century. But that's another story.

Two one-way bridges now span the Missouri, making crossing the river swifter, safer, and easier than once it was for those who walked or bicycled the one 2-way version. The first bridge over the Missouri at this point was a draw bridge, built/begun (dates differ on this) in 1885. The date is firm, however, (1822) when William James first ferried people, stock and cargo over the Mighty Muddy at this point.

Jeff City (as locals call it), a political town, also schmoozes in another county altogether: Cole County. After all, it is the state capital; it strives to succeed as the seat of state government, which it certainly is. This town---for it's a little town, really, and not a capitol "c" city since its population doesn't qualify it as an SMSA (Standard Metropolitan Statistical Area)---this town is named for a high government official, President Thomas

23 KATY TRAIL

Jefferson. Nevertheless, long-term locals often display healthy ambivalence for all things and persons politik; by that we mean, there's little ooou- or ahhh-ing when seeing yet another stretch limo slip down to what is called the "the bottoms," along the boulevard, on its way into the dark recesses of the capitol's tunnel garage.

Whether Jeff Citian (either a Cole or Callaway Countian), most natives here know the Capitol Building, fashioned after the one in D.C., isn't our first. And you must converse with a St. Charlian (east edge of our state) to learn much about "the very first" Missouri State capitol.

Completed in 1826, J.C's first Capitol Building fell to fire in 1837; townsfolk said it wasn't big enough, anyway. The second structure, c. 1840, fell to fire in 1911; it wasn't big enough, also. But the present one (Missouri State Capitol No. 3) evidently not too big for our breeches (yet), erected in 1917---stands today on what some say is Howard's Bluff, overlooking the River. KATY Trail-ers can see the Capitol from far distances.

In the era of flappers, WOS radio broadcasted "fiddle shows" from the Capitol Rotunda, which perpetuated the importance of the fiddle to Missouri. Often the only musical instrument found amid pioneer communities, the fiddle was fiddled at community affairs for dance, jam session, or religious ceremony. Up the trail in Hartsburg, drop in on a fiddle jam-session at the Hitchin' Post. The fiddle was "annointed" as the state instrument in 1987.

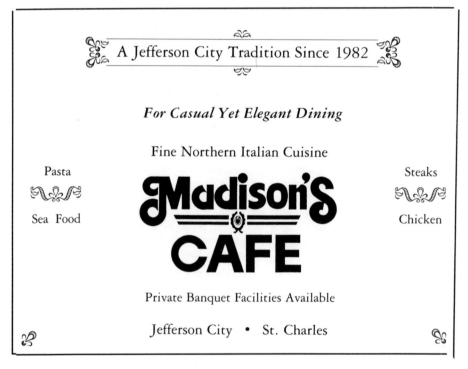

Music can feed the soul, but ya can't eat it. How about combining some great photos of capital fires with a pasta repast? Check the walls of Madison's Cafe (not really a cafe but a restaurant on Madison Street, a block from the Governor's Mansion, just east of the Capitol). Madison's is "becoming a tradition, serving consistently high quality northern Italian cuisine in an elegant yet casual setting."

Or, forget the photos and go around the block for *haut cuisine* (on High Street) at Shawn's River City Grill (grill is a misnomer too). Always busy, New Age Shawn *siestas* daily at 2 but he reopens for dinner fare at 5. Next door to Shawn's on High Street is the wonderful Downtown Book and Toy, where you can buy copies of this Guide for your Grandpa!

On what is called Missouri FastFood Boulevard is another favorite and affordable, writer's pick of culinary pleasure: Pizzaria Napolitana. So much more than pizza! Napolitana offers daily an 11 to 2 buffet and salad bar plus "a full menu of authentic Greek and American food such as prime rib, steak, filet mignon, lamb, seafood, chicken, pasta, with wine or beer from here (Missouri) or elsewhere."

Nearer KATY Trail, in Cedar City territory, on the west side of Hwy 63/54 are the Coffee Cup Cafe (yes, truly a cafe!) and Tremain's Cafe (another one! east side, Jeff City Airport). These local haunts dish-up homestyle breakfast and lunch at reasonable costs; if one isn't open, tuther is.

Jeff City has numerous lodging choices (from cheap to high china) including one bed and breakfast roost.

While in Jeff's historic neighborhood, slip into the Capitol. Of Carthage or Missouri limestone marble, its Neoclassical Roman Renaissance style shows Ceres (goddess of grain) atop its dome, touting the importance of agriculture to Missouri. Ole TJ himself (Thomas Jefferson) in bronze stands in the middle of three massive plateaus of stairway (a climb to get to him). Two entries are at ground level, however, and elevators assist the tired and/or physically challenged KATY-er *tooriste*. On the main level is the State Museum (state history exhibits) and in the legislators' lounge the Thomas Hart Benton mural (telling Missouri's socio-political story with breathtaking beauty and amusing frankness). Lunettes (some 40 or so smaller murals) nitched in arch-spaces of the hallowed corridors allure an artistic eye: Victor Higgins' "The First Steamboat on the Missouri River Arriving at New Franklin in 1819," "Daniel Boone's Sons Making Salt at Boone's Lick," "Lewis and Clark at the Mouth of the Osage River"; Irving Couse's "Log Cabins," "Osage Village," "Osage Hunters." Other "capitol art" signatures: Berninghaus, Dunton, Galt, Miller, N.C. Wyeth, Ufer.

Within a block's walk at Jefferson Landing, Lohman's building (1880s) once functioned as the center of busy commercial river/trail trade. (Charles Lohman's steamboat, the *Viola Belle*, traveled from Great Falls, Montana, to New Orleans.) Union Hotel, built around 1880, and the 1856 Christopher Maus House add their perspective to the budding city. *The Jeffersonian*, founded 1825 by Calvin Gunn, claims fame for being the city's first newspaper. Gunn put his paper to bed on the corner of Madison and Capitol Streets in one of the row houses across from the present Governor's Mansion.

Detail, Benton mural in the legislative lounge of the Missouri state Capitol, with "politikin, baby's bare bottom, hanging/frontier justice, and steamboat"
<u>Walker/Cole County Historical Museum</u> photo.

In this chief executive mansion (1871) *aux jardins* the Governor and his family reside. It's the design of George Ingham Barnett who modelled it after Riverscene, the home with a French-Italian mansard roof built along the Missouri River near Boonville.

The Cole County Historical Museum, located in the Federal-style row house of Benjamin Gratz Brown, faces the Governor's Mansion/Gardens. CCHM's collection displays the opulence of an early era. Much of the furniture in its drawing room was imported from France. Its master bedroom contains a half-tester bed (the canopy may have served to protect its sleepers from falling plaster); the bed's hollow pillars served as a safe. As with most houses of that era, the master bedroom has no closets, for houses were taxed by their number of rooms, and closets were counted as rooms. Cole County Historical Museum preserves a collection of Governors' wives gowns, children's toys and furniture, and the first bicycle in Jefferson City---a true bone shaker.

Otis Manchester, Sr. donated his Singer Ordinaries Bicycle (not the Extra-Ordinaries model) which was built in Defiance, Ohio, at a cost of $150 in 1880. With metal seat and a front wheel size ranging from 42" to 52" driven by turn of crank, the rider pedalled constantly. But real challenges came in pedalling through mud, muck, and on gravel, as well as getting on and off Ordinaries.

Jeff City has cycle shops *cum* rental, repair, or right to ownership. While you're on High Street, so to speak, stop in at Midwest Cycle Sports (116 E. High), if you need a bicycle, a "part" or other supplies.

Lincoln University (Lafayette and Dunklin Streets) offers cultural diversions and attractions, depending upon term and theatrical season. It

27 KATY TRAIL

sponsors concert series and other events common to university life. Established in 1866 "to educate free men," LU is part of University of Missouri.

Back on the trail toward Hartsburg is Cedar Creek; approximately one mile north of Cedar Creek (MP 147.5), you're now in Boone county, named for Dan'l.

Historic Downtown Jefferson City

Missouri Capitol (1917) & Museum
Visitor's Information Desk (314) 751-4127

Jefferson Landing State Historic Site (314) 751-3475
Lohman Building (1830s)
Union Hotel/Elizabeth Rozier gallery (1850s)

Governor's Mansion/Gardens (1826) (314) 751-3222
Tuesday Tours Only

Cole County Historical Museum (314) 635-1850
Upschulte House (1870s)

The Monroe House (1879 43-room hotel)
Monroe & High St.
Now Legal offices

Hope Mercantile Building (1854)
Hides, furs, clothing, groceries, toys
Later a saloon gambling house
122 E. High St.
Now Katie Janes Gifts & Coffee

Louis C. Lohman Store (1870s)
Lohman Opera House
High & Jefferson St.
Now Taco Bell

Elsewhere

Lincoln University (1866)
Lafayette Dunklin St.
Tours/activities: (314) 681-5000

Ordinaries bicycle, in Cole County Historical Museum.

Conservation Department (314) 751-4115
Headquarters/Grounds, 2901 W. Truman
24-hr reservation for guided tours
Self-guided on grounds anytime

JC Parks/Recreation Hotline
(314) 634-6485

Missouri Division of Tourism (314) 751-4133
Truman State Office Bldg. (High & Broadway)

KATY TRAIL 28

Hartsburg (MP 153.6) - Population 130 (or so)

Claysville, Wilton, Spencer, and a few "lost" towns

KATY Trail-ers! There are several lesser-known towns to acquaint yourself with as you trek t'ward Hartsburg. Leaving the Jeff City river bottoms *nee* Cedar City area, KATY Trail moves away from the Missouri River. Going west, trekkers see the river to their left and Ordivician bluffs of dolomite soaring above to the right.

Claysville (MP 149.7) developed as a river town about a mile off the Missouri River. It was named in honor of Henry Clay and opened its first store in 1845.

Entrepreneurship on the Trail, at Claysville. Note the gate in background, reminding KATY Trail-ers: YIELD at crossings.

Steamboats once ported in the community of Claysville (now about six homes) which was settled following the demise of Stonesport, just one mile north, which slipped away during the flood of 1844. Settled by Mat (not Mae) West, Stonesport had been laid out in 1936 by Asa Stone. It has been written that Stonesport aspired to be the state's capital city, but "got flooded under." Westerly was another pre-existing now-extinct town, called Burlington, which, too, went with the 1844 flood. Former Burlingtonian Thaddius Hickman ran a store in Hartsburg c. 1867-75, then turned his attention to breeding thoroughbred shorthorns (cattle). Ribs of a prehistoric animal (a mastodon) were unearthed during an 1860 excavation of this area. Between Soft Pit Hill Road (MP 152.3) and Hartsburg, the Ordivician bluffs of dolomite...

A lazy day in Hartsburg.

Oopps! right-of-way 1/4 *mile*, not meter.

Hartsburg (MP 153.6) developed following Luther D. Hart's donation to the railroad of a needed 1/4th meter of right-of-way for the MKT. The Melbourne Post Office moved to Hartsburg in 1883, and soon the town supported two banks (which merged in 1927, and closed in 1944).

Now that the KATY's "on line," townsfolk say Hartsburg's revitalizing. The 16 miles from Jeff City to Hartsburg is popular with members of the Capitol City Cyclists Club (AKA, 4-C-ers?) and other adventurers-of-Hart. Hartsburg boasts two cafes (yes) and bike rentals. Cyclists reconnoiter for the Friday Spaghetti Run (miles westerly out of/back to Hartsburg), afterwhich they sit and chat, waiting for spagetti, served family style. At the Hitchin' Post on Sundays, usually an audience gathers to hear fiddle playing.

The "look" of Hartsburg is one predominantly styled with Victorian homes built in the late 1800's and early 1900's. Train service to Hartburg began in 1883, and in that same year the Globe Hotel opened (it closed in the 1950's). The Globe is being renovated to serve as an inn. When trains started shipping produce and cattle through, to, and from the town, it began to grow. A half-million dollars of wheat came out of Hartburg in its "hayday," (this, a spell-find to amuse!) and at the time of peak service, in 1953, two passenger trains and 10 freight trains stopped in Hartsburg per day. Today, Hartsburg's proud of being the pumpkin capitol of Missouri.

Easing out of Hartsburg, KATY Trail passes again through rich river bottom land. North of Hart Creek (MP 154.5) the bluffs reach almost 150-foot heights. In another mile, KATY Trail parallels the Missouri River.

Bluffs run along Hartsburg and Wilton (MP 157.4). Lewis and Clark camped at Wilton on June 4, 1804. (Folks say Wilton rose from the ashes of Spencer. Where's Spencer? a ha' mile south a here.) In 1882, a prospector from Colorado formed the Boone County Gold Company, claiming he discovered gold and silver near Wilton. Although a river landing in this area was called "Eureka," mining excavations produced more lead than either of these precious metals. An immigrant cemetery (small pox fatalities) is in this area; a brick home dating 1839 was erected in the now defunct town of Spencer.

At Hagan's Landing, one 1880s merchant specialized in shipping railroad ties, about 20,000 per year. The Goshen Church, located off M on Cedar Tree Road, was organized in 1832, but the current building dates in at 1875.

The Missouri River curves close to KATY Trail at Bonne Femme Creek (MP 161.6); from here to north Easley, small house trailers and cottages line the river banks. Some are permanent, some used only as recreational cabins: fishing, swimming, canoeing.

Fall pumpkin harvest in Hartsburg area.

A faint moon above the Trail, south of Hartsburg.

KATY TRAIL 32

This log cabin, typical of early- to mid-1800s, may have been the meeting place for the formation of the Goshen Church in Wilton, 1832.

Easley Township (MP 162.3) - Boone County

Providence, 1-of-2 Petersburgs, Nashville "lost" towns

The Easley "caves" (MP 162.2) which resulted from mining for rock-wool (for insulation) can be seen on the east side of the bluffs. Please respect the blockaid to the road leading to the bluffs. Dolomite, transported across the road via pipes to a melting site, was transformed into rock-wool here and then shipped down the river.

In a nutshell, it was Easley's General Store (1891) that created the community of Easley. This store is a "must stop" for any self-respecting bicylist, hiker, walker. If you arrive by road rather than trail, check your foot brakes and brace yourself, for "the hill" in Easley ain't easy, it's steep! Sign sez "Slow Carp Crossing." Enjoy hamburgers or chicken breast sandwiches made at Easley's, in the grassy picnic area off the trail and near the store or stand inside near the pot-bellied stove. Snacks, frozen yogurt, cider, and a KATY Guide writer's favorite (Schwann's Sundae Cone) are available at Easley's. On cool days, KATY-ers will want the warmth of Easley's wood burning stove. Easley's decor? photos of some of her floods and one of an MKT train "passing on April 5, 1986, five days before the line was discontinued." Easley's Store grocers the community, and rents bicycles-built for two and those for one.

33 KATY TRAIL

From Easley to McBaine (MP 169.4) is a short 7.1 mile trek. At the point where the river curves west away from the trail (MP 164) was the once-upon-a-town of Nashville. What remains of the town can be seen from KATY Trail. Nashville was named for Ira P. Nash, the first white settler in this area; Nash received this land via land grant from the Spanish (pre-Louisiana Purchase). Nash, "an eccentric genius...the most quarrelsome man in Missouri," gave orders to be buried on the bluffs in a standing position "so he could look down on his neighbors."

In 1820, Nashville had a tobacco warehouse and its own post office. It once was a major shipping point, until its northern neighbor Rocheport began to burgeon. Nashville washed away in 1844; waters flowed over it eight foot high.

Providence (MP 165.3) arose after Nashville washed away. James Audubon collected specimens and sketched wildlife along the Missouri River, and stayed over in a Hotel in Providence. The town of Providence once had fine hotels, elegant residences; a grocery and two general stores, though one Providencian was both "mechanic and undertaker, and Robert Nivens plies the art of Vulcan." Formal balls took place in Providence. Just north of Old Plank Road, Providence's stone walls are visible, to the east. These walls were for ornament, to protect and backdrop Providence's flower gardens. The 10-mile Old Plank Road which led to Columbia in the 1850s was made of oak sills. Near Providence to the west, between Perche Creek and the river, two towns once thrived so that George Sexton ran several miles of mail route service. One of the towns, Petersburg, laid out in 1836 "was known mostly for its horse racing, whiskey, drinking, and fighting."

Little Bonne Femme Creek meets the Missouri River north of Easley.

KATY TRAIL 34

MKT logo and springs (don't drink the water!); it's only a few more minutes to Rocheport where you can get refreshed.

Original rail mile marker north of Providence.
The MP signs on the KATY correspond to the original railroad mileage.

McBaine Township (MP 169.4)
Boone County

Huntsdale

*fiqure as sketched
in the Original Journal.*

Courtesy DNR

    The little town of McBaine developed much later than most of the towns along the trail thus far. In 1911, the MKT Railroad named McBaine for the "owners of large farms that operated the grain elevator along the tracks." The town was being settled in the 1890's by tenant farmers. There remains one (count it) place of business in McBaine where a person can wet a whistle and put on a feed bag: at the Hideaway (.2 miles off the Trail) it's "Beer, Soda, Ice, Pool" (as in billiards). Ya can't miss it, unless you miss McBaine.

    The 8.5 miles of railroad spur from McBaine to Columbia is being developed by Boone County and the City of Columbia with intent to connect with McBaine. A 4-mile area extending southwest from downtown Columbia has been completed; at present, Boone County planners still are at work on this trail connection which will add a nice side trip for KATY Trail-ers. The first two miles will traverse through farm land. Going west at Burr Oak Road (MP 170.8) for .15 miles are two burr oak trees, the largest, that is, having the largest diameter of any burr oak in the state.

    Huntsdale (MP 171.6) was also founded as a railroad town. No services in Huntsdale, so don't hunt for 'em.

    The Burlington limestone bluffs north of Huntsdale were once called the Big Moniteau Bluffs. Lewis and Clark noted the pictographs in their journals: "The pictured rocks" or "the Indian pictographs of Boone County" included "two crudely executed drawings of human figures, perhaps 20" in height with arms extended; one small human figure with a staff in its hand; numerous circles, with dots and crosses in the centre; spots within semi-circles, half-resembling the human eye."

    June 6, 1804 writings of Lewis and Clark note the "uncouth paintings of animals...white, red, and blue flint" and indicated that the site was infested with rattlesnakes. Maximilliam, Prince of Wied, commented on the "red figures on the rocky walls" when he traveled the area in 1833. Unfortunately, the builders of the MKT destroyed most of these drawings. One still exists above the Lewis and Clark Cave. KATY Trail's entrance to Boone Cave is at MP 174.9. This cave "with its large rooms" was described by Switzer in 1882 as Sinking Creek Cave.

    Another cave farther west has a wooden door on huge iron hinges. Some say Jesse James hid out in this cave; others say the cave was used as a storehouse for powder and shot for Civil War Confederates, particularly addressing the Battle of Lexington. MKT Railroad personnel probably used the cave for storing building supplies.

Eagle Bluffs Wildlife Area (MP 169) - Boone County

   KATY Trail parallels the Eagle Bluffs Wildlife Area located a few miles south of McBaine (and seven miles southwest of Columbia). It is one of two Missouri wetlands within range of this 50-mile section of the Trail. KATY-ers will see marshes lush with cattails, bulrushes, and native grasses accessed by Eagle Bluffs Wildlife Area walkways. Planners of this wildlife area designated an "accessible overlook" for people who use wheelchairs.

   Eagle Bluff's wetlands are husbanded jointly by the Missouri Department of Conservation and the City of Columbia. Eagle Bluffs Wildlife Area provides a home or resting place for birds and migratory waterfowl (bald eagle, turkey vultures, Canada geese, blue winged teal, wood ducks great blue herons, etc.). Consequently, its atmosphere is full with the beauty of silence---broken by frequent birdsong. Remains of Native American encampments were unearthed when this manmade wildlife area was constructed.

   Spanning 2700 acres, Eagle Bluffs Wildlife Area also is an essential component of the largest natural wastewater treatment wetland in the United States. The August 1991 *Missouri Conservation* notes that the City of Columbia pipes its wastewater after it's been treated into this wetland labyrinth of marsh and stream, and that sewage flows from Columbia to a conventional treatment plant, then to a series of wetland treatment cells. Eagle Bluffs Wildlife Area receives 12 to 20 million gallons of high quality water from these cells. This waterworks network connects with and flows to its destination, the Missouri River.

Perche Creek in the Eagle Bluffs Wildlife Area.

Rocheport c. 1895. Note MKT Depot and rail dominance.
Photo courtesy of Friends of Rocheport Museum.

Rocheport (MP 178.3) - Population 273
Elevation 596' - Boone County

Rocheport (port of rocks) "originated" after Missouri's New Madrid earthquake of 1818. People in the southeastern part of the state (near the quake's epi-center where farmlands disappeared and terrain shifted) migrated upland; they were gifted with equivalent grants of land in Rocheport and other parts of Boonslick Country.

In 1825, Rocheport was platted on 191 acres and it soon became an important shipping town whose businesses rivaled those of nearby Columbia. Its claim in history is that of being a key shipping point between St. Louis and St. Joseph, and one of the major crossings for Boone's Lick Road. Congress in 1827, established a post road "from Fulton by Columbia, Rockport [Rocheport], Booneville (sic)" and later, Rocheport had a ferry crossing on the National Old Trails Road. Ten years later, a horse-pulled ferry brought more trade through the area. Selling ice proved lucrative for Rocheportians, who, in the winter time, cut ice from the Missouri River and Moniteau Creek and stored it in ice houses. Insulated with sawdust and straw, the ice held through to the summer. One ice house (15-sq. by 20-ft deep) still remains in Rocheport, thanks to restoration work by the Friends of Rocheport. The ice house roof is steeply pitched to accommodate a pulley used to lift out heavy blocks of ice.

But farming and grist milling were main sources of industry for Rocheportians, who shipped 15,000 lbs of flour per year to St. Louis. Tobacco, also a major crop ship-loaded out of Rocheport, provided sizeable incomes for several t'backy farmers.

Rocheportians even enjoyed the tourist trade of steamboat holiday excursions. The 1825 Linden Lake Chautauqua at the Roby Farm became one of the earliest Chautauquas in the country.

Exposed to a mix of traffic, this center of trade carried the diseases of the day to its residents. Many Rocheportians felt the blows of cholera epidemics that hit the town in 1833, 1849, and again in 1852. This commerical river town also endured several major floods as the Missouri River and surrounding creeks exceeded their levels in 1844, 1849, and 1852. Water reached the second floor of many downtown buildings during the great and awful flood of '44.

When war pitted brother against brother, many Boone Countians sympathized with the Confederacy. Governor Claiborne Jackson favored secession, but during a special convention, folks cast votes to go with the Union. Former governor Sterling Price led 50,000 state militia volunteers (called by Jackson to join confederate soldiers at Boonville) and Bill Anderson and his bushwackers claimed Rocheport as their capitol in September 1864. When Union soldiers marched on Rocheport, they torched much of it.

But it was a "natural" fire of 1922 that leveled many of the buildings of reconstructed Rocheport; few, consequently, predate 1922. The pre-1840 home of river captain John Keiser survived fires, floods, and other furies. It stands on the corner of Central and Second.

Also of note is the fact that the Whig party held its state convention in Rocheport in June 1840. Estimates vary widely as to attendance numbers, from six to 10,000. Since the state's population at that time was less than 400,000, these "estimates" attest to the perceptions of Whig participants and their opponents. Although no historical evidence or document exists to support such, it is said that Abraham Lincoln attended this convention. Some records show that Honest Abe was courting Mary Todd in nearby Columbia (Missouri) about this time.

Rocheport Ferry. Photo courtesy of Friends of Rocheport Museum.

The ice house, a reminder of business past, was restored by the Friends of Rocheport.

After the Civil War, Rocheportians strove to revive themselves and their town. One of the first telephone lines in Missouri was built from Columbia to Rocheport (1878). And in 1892, the Missouri-Kansas-Texas Railroad rolled its iron feet in Rocheport. Hugo Dietrich, a legendary Rocheportian, won first place as the fastest straight-edge man in the 1904 World Fair (Meet Me in St. Louie, Louie). One long-winded story reveals how, as a train smoked through Rocheport, this railroad brakeman jumped from the front of the train to get a shave, and climbed back onto its caboose clean-shaven!

And Willie Clark referred to Rocheport, noting "white red and blue flint" paintings and carvings, and he wrote that he discovered a den of rattlesnakes in the area.

Rocheport received placement on the National Register of Historic Places in 1976. Friends of Rocheport opened its museum in 1973 in a restored 1840s store, and maintains a worthwhile collection of quilts, clothing, and other artifacts from the area.

Rocheport has two areas of attraction and services: downtown Rocheport and Missouri River City. Located on both sides of I-70 interchange, MRC is 2 miles on Hwy BB south from town. Both areas have fine antique stores, restaurants, lodging including a bed and breakfast, some craft stores, bicycle rentals, and a winery. The area is a budding haven for fine arts and crafts people, also. Just as you reach Rocheport, you will pass a white church which is currently being restored to its pre-Civil War look. The Mt. Nebo Baptist Church, built by black slaves for their use, soon will open as an art gallery and deli.

Mt. Nebo Church, prior to restoration. The church was built prior to Civil War by slaves for their use.

Tour and/or taste? Try Les Bourgeois Wineries and Bistro, a popular outdoor setting *avec* umbrella-ed tables and views overlooking the river.

Flavors of the Heartland store in Missouri River City offers "gourmet foods, original art and handcrafted items, custom gift baskets, and antiques in an authentic 1800s log cabin."

Want to stay overnight? Try the School House Bed and Breakfast (314) 698-2022, also a source of local info.

Rocheportians and the Department of Natural Resources are working together to rebuild the train depot to have public restrooms, a meeting room, information center. It may be open by the time this book is published.

Notice Moniteau Creek. Moniteau means Great Spririt or Deity in the language of Native Americans that lived in the area. Also of note is (just north of Rocheport) the only tunnel on the MKT line, a tunnel of 240-feet.

Columbia Audubon Society (314) 474-3272

Friends of Rocheport (314) 698-4074

School House Bed and Breakfast (314) 698-2022

Les Bourgeois Wineries & Bistro (314) 698-3401

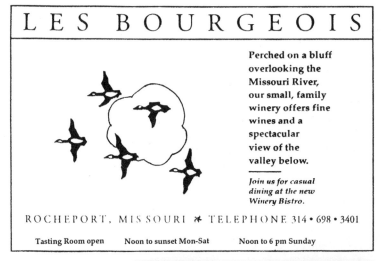

MKT tunnel, west of Rocheport, is the only tunnel on the MKT line. Notice footsteps and bicycle tracks in the snow...

Davisdale Wildlife Area (MP 181.4 - 183.1) - Howard County

Seven miles east of Boonville, the Davisdale Wildlife Area spans 2400 acres of timber, ponds, croplands, and native Missouri warm and cool-season grassland (bluestem and Indian grasses, for example).

Two entrances to this Wildlife Area exist from the KATY Trail. The east entrance is approximately 1/8th mile north of Highway 40; the second entrance is about a half mile west of the east entrance.

The Department of Conservation maintains approximately nine miles of hiking trails in Davisdale Wildlife Area (lush with flora and fauna, deer, turkey, quail, and songbirds) and regulates public deer hunting, fishing, trapping, and allows picking of mushroom, berries and fruits in this area. According to a state flier: "Davisdale has at least three Indian mounds as well as history of early English settlers. Its topography and habitat make it a unique and productive tract."

Questions concerning Davisdale can be answered by calling Columbia's Conservation office: (314) 882-9880.

Here and there a little meadow water-course is golden with marsh marigolds...

John Burroughs
from Signs and Seasons

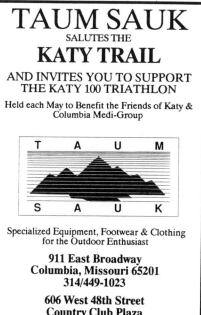

Cold sweet air, tingling sun and freezing shade...Lace patterns on the snow of pine needles, frangrance of fallen boughs, old wood! These are the words of the earth.

Cedric Wright
from "Trail Song"

(Old & New) Franklin (MP 188.3) - Population 1,107 Elevation 596' at trail head - Howard County

Over time, folks said they saw many a scalawag and river rat floating through Franklin. The 1826-30 Missouri River floods devastated (washed out and away) the town. New Franklin was platted in 1828 several miles "further down the trail." New Franklin's principal growth, however, was "furthered" by the MKT railroad junction, one mile west.

The Santa Fe Trail began in Franklin in 1821. This marker, on west side of Hwy 87 at the Trail, is the site of Old Franklin (which washed away with the flood of 1826).

Cement steps along the Trail lead to Hwy 5 and to New Franklin.

A MKT caboose is being refurbished for placement along the trail in New Franklin, whose downtown offers benches for "just soaking up local color."

Yes, Virginia, it's true. The Santa Fe Trail began in this once-forgotten town. The Santa Fe Trail thrived for 50 years in this region of Missouri. She created migration patterns that brought much commerce into this state. William Becknell organized the Santa Fe Trail Trade Company, advertising his venture in the *Intelligencer* in 1821 "for purpose of trading hopes and mules, catching wild animals...for the benefit of the company."

Becknell and his men left Franklin and traveled 900 miles from

September 1 to November 16 that first year, trading merchandise all along the trail. Merchandise they returned to Franklin with was valued at $3,000. In 1822 with 21 men, he led three trips to Santa Fe in 45 days. The town of (Ben) Franklin fame had become known as "the" outfitting post along the Santa Fe Trail. By 1824, trading parties along the trail numbered 25 wagons, 30 men, and 150 horses. Prairie schooner wagons sported flared bows, sterns and 7' diameter wheels. The largest trip (in 1830) tallied over 200 men who returned with goods and silver valued at $270,000. Profits from these trail runs ran as high as two thousand percent. Wagon trails carried:

"cutlery, silk shawls, looking glasses, cotton goods, callicos, handkerchiefs, woolen goods, crepes, bolts of velvet, knives, traps, boxes of beads and trinkets for the Indians and scores of other articles."

These often were traded for silver coin, mules, and wool. Two-way trade along the Santa Fe Trail helped the country recover from the economic drag of 1819. Missouri goods were shipped to Santa Fe in about five to six weeks' time. Approximately 90 merchants made $3 million profit in Missouri between 1822 and 1843. It was via Santa Fe Trail trading that Missouri acquired the mule (a result of crossing the Santa Fe jackass with a she horse) for which Missouri is famous.

The expanse of the Santa Fe Trail can be seen from the hill of Clark Chapel Church and Cemetery (off Hwy 87). With the 1826 Franklin flood, the trail head moved to Boonville for a year, then to Arrow Rock, and then further west to the Kansas City area.

The Pearson's Grain Elevator c. 1920, on the Trail near New Franklin.

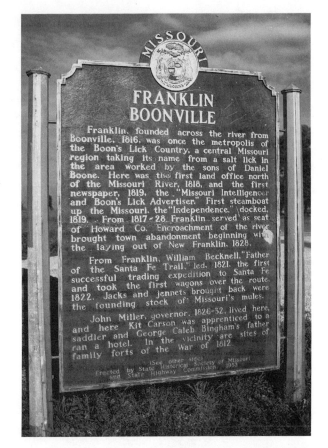

Boonslick commerce was important to economic development of Missouri and The West.

While at Clark's Chapel, listen for the haunt of "Gray Ghost," the spirit of Richard M. Kimzey. Kimzey, a member of Quantrill's Civil War guerillas, is buried in this cemetery. History texts say townsfolk feared and hated Kimzey, who took what he wanted and killed people at whim. On October 8, 1864, Confederate Captain Bill Quantrill on horseback met Kimzey "on a high road west of Clark's Chapel" and shot the rogue. The two men had arranged to meet there, for Quantrill had received reports of Kimzey's atrocities, and planned to dismiss Kimzey from his regiment.

New Franklineans thought that their 1990 effort of "rest-orating" Kimzey's grave marker put an end to the echoing cries of his voice ("Kim-zee, Kim-zee") and the staccato noise of his horse's hoofs clapping down the hollers of this rugged countryside. But it hasn't worked.

Other famous Franklin residents are George Caleb Bingham (who lived there when he was a boy) and Christopher Columbus Carson, better known as Kit Carson (the 16 year-old apprentice to a saddle-maker who fled to Santa Fe).

Members of the South Howard County Historical Society and Visitor Center (101 E. Broadway) are working toward having the Franklin area receive acknowledgement of being the beginning of the Santa Fe Trail. The Society sponsors the Santa Fe Trail Day celebration of the history spurred in this little town.

The 1832 Old Seminary (110 Market St.) of brick Federal Style is now a private home. It once served as a two-room school to which parents paid $2.50 monthly to send a child to learn the three Rs, and then some.

Harris-Chilton House (108 N. Missouri Ave.) is a two-story Federal square brick with a one-story ell that was built in 1832 for "a hatter" named Peter B. Harris, and later bought by a New Franklin postmaster, J. W. Chilton.

George Edwards Home, c. 1830 (311 Edwards St.) is a two-story brick residence that Edwards purchased along with 360 acres in 1851.

The Thomas Hickman Farm (west of New Franklin on Broadway) is part of the University of Missouri Experimental Horticultural Research Facility. The 1819 Hickman farmhouse is one of the oldest standing brick farm homes west of the Mississippi. It boasts a 10 acre formal Elizabethan garden. The farm's original gardens ("vine clad, rose-covered bower with serpentine walks paved with shells") were swept away with the flood of...

Also of historical interest is the home of Lee Edgar Settle (114 N. Howard Ave.), composer of "Missouri Waltz" (Missouri's state song). John Beauchamp Jones, a storekeeper of businesses in New Franklin and Arrow Rock, authored *Wild Western Scenes*, 1841, from his Franklin home.

Other sites of interest: Grabe House-1880's (206 N. Missouri Ave.): Laughlin House-1883 (109 W. Broadway); Glover House-1840 (203 E. Broadway); Carpenter House-1857 (204 E. Broadway); Heath Inn-1850 (207 E. Broadway).

Leaving New Franklin, KATY-ers will pass the MKT train station at Franklin junction, then pass several auto salvage companies---

Locals identify the area near the Site of Old Franklin as Kingsbury Siding (essentially a grain elevator and one-time railroad shipping point). It's near a parking lot which is now approximately 700' northeast of erstwhile Old Franklin Public Square. Across Highway 87 is the former location of Franklin, namesake of notorious kite-flyer and founding father-*extraordinaire* Ben Franklin. A marker describes Franklin's bustling years. The town claims to be the site of the first newspaper (*The Missouri Intelligencer*, later named The *Boonslick Advertiser*) west of the Mississippi. Alphonso Wetmore described Missouri life, using the psuedonym of Aurora Borealis. The steamboat *Independence* chugged over to Franklin, May of 1819. The newspapers and the steamboat greatly encouraged the development of Boonslick Country. By 1820, a stage coach line regularly ran to and from St. Louis and Franklin.

KATY Trail-ers *voyageur moderne*, trail-ing onward to Boonville proper must proceed south on Route 87 and cross over the vehicle and pedestrian bridge, rather than the KATY Trail bridge which remains "up" to accommodate river traffic. Some Boonvillians hope that KATY Trail planners will be able to "tie-in" this bridge at some future date.

Then there's Snoddy's Store, a Boonslick legend at the intersection of Highways 40 and 87. At Snoddy's, KATY Trail-ers can pause for refreshments. Snoddy's (don't you love the name?), Snoddy's opened near the site of Cooper's Fort in 1921 and moved into its current home in 1924. When the town's new vehicle and pedestrian bridge is completed in 1993, Snoddy's will relocate again. Currently, Snoddy's maintains the old-fashioned general mercantile approach, similar to the period of time in which C.C. Snoddy first "opened-up" for customers, but with a few modern conveniences (refrigerators, freezers, gas pumps).

If Snoddy's don't have it, maybe ya don't need it.

South Howard County Historical Society/Visitor Ctr.
101 E. Broadway, New Franklin

Welcome to **KATY TRAIL** STATE PARK

As the TRAIL was conceived by the late Edward D. Jones to be a select part of nature to be enjoyed by everyone, so is the purpose of:

 PROMOTIONS ... to make available to Biker/Hiker products to enhance the enjoyment of the TRAIL.

Look for this Label ...
and be assured of a quality product and know that you are helping to support the future of the TRAIL.

Special Note:
All T-Shirts/Sweats have scenes from along the TRAIL- collect them ... Great Rememberances!

"available all along the TRAIL"

 PROMOTIONS

Distributed by: Oliver World Trade Inc.

Boone's Lick
State Historic Site

Howard County

Remains of a salt mine at Boone's Lick State Historic Site. Whitish residue of these saline springs was mined by Boone's sons in the early 1800s.

This unusual attraction, located northwest of Boonesboro, Missouri, is nine miles northwest of the KATY Trail. The Boone's Lick State Historic Site has picnic areas, hiking trails, and rustic "necessary" conveniences known as pit toilets. This 17 acre site contains the remnants of the once thriving salt mining industry gleaned from a natural salt-water spring. Accessed at Highway 87, travel west a few miles on Highway 187, which leads into the site parking area. Both highways leading to this site are hilly, curvy, and narrow, very challenging for bicyclists and those who enjoy lengthy roadside walks. Another route (less traffic, less challenge) which offers gradual rises and falls (oops!) engages Route Z through Petersburg (one of two Petersburgs on this section of the trail). This northern Petersburg has two old cemeteries. County Road J leads directly into Boonesboro.

The area of Boone's Lick State Historical Site was prime for development during the early 1800's. The land was fertile (due to occasional river flooding) for raising crops or raising livestock; its rolling hills verdant with timber were ripe for building needs and the Missouri River offered key inlets. The area supported residents as early as 5000 years ago. Oral tradition credits Daniel Boone with finding this salt lick, although his sons Nathan and Daniel Morgan Boone claim that their father did not discover it.

This salt lick is in a location where Native Americans and pioneers hunted deer that frequented the nurturing minerals. James and Jesse Morrison and Dan'el's sons mined the salt lick from 1806 to 1833. Four miles of land were cleared of timber for the salt industry which, at one time, functioned with four furnaces. Twenty men working rows of bubbling kettles and cauldrons produced 100 bushels of salt (one bushel equalled 50 pounds) and shipped it down the Missouri in piroques and keelboats.

Salt was used in preserving meat and other foods, and for pickling purposes, not porpoises (say that 10 times, if you can!). Much salt, of course, was needed to cure and tan hides. For example, four pounds of salt preserved 20 pounds of ham and a hide required salt equalling one third of its weight. In the early 1800's, salt sold for $2 to $2.50 per bushel.

Daughters of American Revolution marker for Boone's Lick.

Fort Cooper - Howard County

The site of Benjamin Cooper's Fort established during the War of 1812 is about a half mile off a gravel road (County Road 330) from Petersburg (also known as Cooper's Chapel).

The governor ordered area residents to St. Louis during that warfare; those refusing to leave their homes helped build Fort Cooper. Commander Cooper's niece Milly (what's her last name?) is credited as being the first female in American military history. In order to get help from a neighboring fort, Milly charged her horse through the group of Native Americans who had surrounded the fort. The site is marked with a plaque showing a design of the fort and giving some of its history.

A Santa Fe Trail marker is just south (or somewhat KATY-warnpus) of Fort Cooper.

To get to the site of Fort Cooper, proceed north on Highway 87 two miles; turn west on Route Z and travel seven miles to Petersburg.

Two sister fort sites within a 10 mile radius are Ft. Kincaid and Ft. Hempstead.

Boonville (MP 190.6) - Population 7,095
Elevation 675' at trail head - Cooper County

The bridge at Boonville crossing the Missouri River opened for use in 1924. Prior to that date, Boonvillians ferry-boated shore to shore. While crossing the Missouri River, take a look at the Missouri-Kansas-Texas railroad bridge which, when built in 1930, was known for having the longest lift span (480 feet) in the country. Under the vehicle bridge (not the MKT bridge) is a cobblestone road, the first paved road west of St. Louis, created in 1832 with the sweat of slave labor.

Katy Station Depot, with its original, distinctive red tile roof, is the only Spanish-style depot remaining along "the Katy Line." The Department of Natural Resources nominated this depot for inclusion on the National Register of Historic Sites, with plans to restore it. The depot's red tiles are in storage at the time of this writing. With the decline of passenger train use, by 1969 most stations closed shop. The tracks of the Katy (then Tebo and Neosho Railway) reached Boonville on June 31, 1873. On the Fourth of July that year, Boonvillians celebrated the occasion of the Northeastern Extension from Sedalia to Hannibal. Train cars ferried across the Missouri River until 1874, when a draw bridge serviced the railroad.

The bridge across the Missouri in Boonville, c. 1924. KATY bridge in background (with its 480' lift span "up") was built in 1930.

Hannah Cole (one of the first white settlers in Boonville) came here in 1810. She was a widow with nine kids. Hannah made her reputation as the operator of the first ferry business in Boonville.

When hostilities between Native Americans and white settlers escalated, the timid and the brave of heart scrambled together to establish fortification against "the barbarous Indians." They erected a fort near what is now the 1200 block of Morgan Street. The fort was appropriated for exhibits in 1853 and 1854 by the state's Agricultural Society. A small marker for the Hannah Cole Fort Site can be found at 1200 Morgan Street.

A place of "encampment affording [good] food and water" is Boonville's best Bed and Breakfast Lady Goldenrod Inn. This turn-of-the-century Queen Anne B & B is the home of innkeepers Chef George and wife Lica and their children. Located in historic Boonville proper, this 3-story original was the home of Thomas Hogan, responsible for Boonville's first brick street and the city's water works. Designed by Hogan, the staircase is intact as are other appointments faithful to his era. The Teddy-on-a-bicycle Bathroom and Tea/Sitting Room add their own kind of ambience.

But don't overlook Bobber's. Bobber Auto/Truck Plaza and Campground has camping sites ('cept during winter) with full hook-ups for RVs and sites for tents, neighboring showers and rest rooms. The food at Bobber's Restaurant is good, especially the pies; service friendly and efficient.

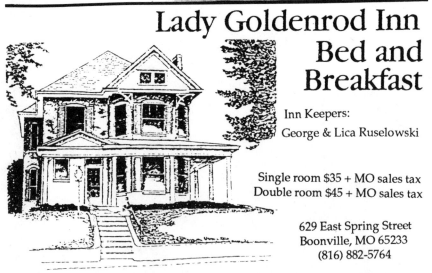

Lady Goldenrod Inn
Bed and
Breakfast

Inn Keepers:

George & Lica Ruselowski

Single room $35 + MO sales tax
Double room $45 + MO sales tax

629 East Spring Street
Boonville, MO 65233
(816) 882-5764

Queen Anne style home with wide veranda and bay windows, Lady Goldenrod Inn Bed & Breakfast is a lovingly preserved turn-of-the-century home. Antiques grace the hallways and living areas. The upstairs bathroom, shared by host and guests, has a stained wood floor and the original claw-foot bath tub.

Home cooking of Chef George of the Country Club of Missouri and Lica's big smile adds to the charm of this quaint bed and breakfast.

MKT caboose stationed by Boonville Depot.

Boonville's Civil War history is noteworthy. Located on the Missouri River, Boonville became a strategic pawn frought with opposing forces. One month before the battle of Bull Run, Union General Nathaniel Lyon defeated Missouri Confederates (led by Governor Claiborne Jackson) on   June 17, 1861, keeping Missouri in the Union and the Missouri River under Union control. Another battle of note is referred to as "the capture of Boonville" when General Sterling Price rampaged through Boonville, October 14, 1864.

In the 1830s, business in Boonville varied. Moore and Porter's saddle company set up shop in 1839. By 1850, the area had become a milling center. Some hundred years later, with the Phoenix-American Factory claiming Boonville as its headquarters, the town had a brief tenure

Boonville Depot, spanish-styled with red tile roof.

The headquarters of the Missouri State Society of the Daughters of the American Revolution.

as "The Corn Cob Pipe Capitol of the World." Those interested in pipe history and pipe dreams can consult Christopher Morley's essay about this little Boonville industry that went up in smoke in 1953.

Boonville, once profuse with grape arbors, produced 6000 gallons of wine in the year of 1859. Consequently, she vintaged the nickname of "The Vine Clad City," which now a local garden club uses in its name. Well, it was an off-shoot of a railroad man, Chief Engineer Edward Miller of the Pacific-Missouri Railroad, hoping to compete with the alcoholic beverages made from grain stills fragrancing the area. Miller sold barrels and barrels of his wine, produced from what he thought to be perfect grape growing country, this Upland Ozark terrain that met western prairies near the overland route called the Santa Fe Trail.

Present-day Boonvillians live amid a diversity of architectural styles. The 1871 Presbyterian Church (417 Vine St.) is a "baroque fantasy." With restorations underway as we write this guidebook, The Ballantine House (409 E. High) stands as one of the oldest buildings in Boonville. The earliest part of The Ballentine inclusive of its two additions dates c. 1820. The 12-room palatial dwelling of Wilbur and wife Rhoda Stephens Johnson known as Roslyn Heights (821 Main St.), constructed in Queen Anne style in the Gay Nineties with touches of Romanesque Revival architecture is the state headquarters of the D.A.R. And Boonville's early history professes

Corn harvest, along the Trail.
Other crops which Trail-ers will see: soybeans, sorghum, winter wheat.

it to be a progressive school town. The Missouri Female Seminary (AKA Aldelphae College) functioned prior to the Civil War. Kemper (AKA New Boonville) Military Academy, founded in 1844, is the oldest boys' school west of the Mississippi, and touts ole Will Rogers as one of its graduates. And the dear lassie Julia Megquire founded her school for young ladies in 1892, specializing in music, but she closed its doors thirteen years later.

But Boonville's enduring pride falls to Thespian Hall. Dedicated on July Fourth in 1857, the Greek Revival Classic records herself as the oldest theatre west of the Allegheny Mountains. Thespians, however, had emerged by 1838. Play bills stopped flying when civil war thunder shook the land, at which time Thespian Hall served as a hospital, a prison, and barracks. Touring theatre troups eventually re-took the Hall; and when "the flicks" came on the scene early in the 20th Century, Boonvillians watched silent movies at Thespian Hall, with piano accompaniment!

Friends of Historic Boonville began restoration of the theatre in 1975. Now, Friends host the annual Missouri River Festival of the Arts (concerts, ballets, plays, puppet shows, etc.). Thespian Hall, placed on the National Register of Historic Places, seats a little less than 700 theatre goers, but is known for superior acoustics.

To get to Harley Park Lookout Point, take Morgan Street west about a third of a mile to Parkway Drive. This respite provides a good overview of the Santa Fe Trail and a haven for RVs. With hook-ups for camping facilities, this 20-acre park dates to 1887. Of particular interest are four burial mounds identified in a city brochure as Hopewell Indian (Middle Woodland 500 BC - 400 AD). Other literature says they are of Lake Woodland period (400 AD - 900 AD). The mounds are on the National Register of Historic Places.

KATY TRAIL 60

The Cooper County Jail/Hanging Barn and Sheriff's Residence are open to the public for tours. The 1836 Swiss German Hain House/Memorial Garden can be toured and/or rented by individuals and groups for social events, exhibits, and meetings.

A riverboat baron, the inventor of the stern paddle principle, friend of George Caleb Bingham, and founder of Kinney Shoes Company spent five years building Riverscene. It's an 11-room mansion just north of the Missouri River. From 1864 to 1869, Captain Joseph Kinney and wife Matilda supervised the acquisition of choice logs and imported Italian marble (used to embellish nine fireplaces), to oversee the cedar flooring of their dance-parlor and the hand-carved contruction (without nails) of a grand mahogany stairway and the making of black walnut doors for their magnificently appointed mansard-roof residence. Captain Kinney's lavishly appointed steamboats carried 300 to 400 persons who paid a competitive price to the Stage Coach fare of $10.50 to travel St. Louis/Boonville. Boonslick Road ran in front of the Captain's mansion. A few years after Riverscene was built, state government used Kinney's plans to construct the present governor's mansion in Jeff City.

At the age of 12, George Caleb Bingham apprenticed himself to a Cooper County cabinet maker and carpenter. Bingham's summer residence, called Forest Hill (700 10th St.) contains one of his paintings.

And not too distant in Cooper County in the Bell Air community (AKA Little Dixie) is Ravenswood. Set amid 1,900 acres, Ravenswood displays 1880s opulence in Capt. Charles Leonard's home (Hwy 5 north from Hwy 50, south of Boonville a few miles).

Boonslick Historical Society, 511 Sixth St.

**Boonville Chamber of Commerce - (816) 882-2721
200 Main St.**

**Thespian Hall/Friends of Historic Boonville
522 Main St. - (816) 882-7977**

BORGMAN'S BED & BREAKFAST

Arrow Rock, Mo.
816-837-3350
Kathy & Helen Borgman

No Smoking
$40 - $50

KATY TRAIL 62

Arrow Rock - Population 80
Elevation 650' - Saline County

KATY Trail cyclists in Arrow Rock.

To get to Arrow Rock from Boonville, take Highways 40 and 5 (Ashley Road toward) I-70. Turn west at Sportsman Road which, in four miles, becomes Highway 41. Go northwest 13 miles on Highway 41 to reach Arrow Rock.

A small community, retaining much of its 19th century flavor and Boonslick Country history, Arrow Rock nestles atop a Missouri River bluff. Arrow Rock is in Saline County, a county named not for a pioneer, politician or other person "of importance," but for its many saline springs. Arrow Rock is north of Lamine River (named by the French explorer Dumont de Montigny) and legend has it that an arrow, embedded in the bluff by an Indian warrior who competed for a tribal chief's daughter, led to the name Pierre à Flèche. On 18th century maps used by French explorers, the words translate into English as "Arrow Rock." In frontier jargon, it sometimes was called 'Airy Rock.' Archaeological evidence supports the presumption of prehistoric habitation in the area, and of Arrow Rock being a gathering place for Native Americans who harvested flint stone (from which to make arrow heads).

Friends of Arrow Rock, a not-for-profit group founded 1959, preserved much of the history of this town which is now a State Historic Site managed by the Department of Natural Resources. Lewis and Clark passed by Arrow Rock, June 9, 1804, and wrote: "a handsome spot for a town."

The earliest white settler, George Sibley, set up a trading post in 1813 in Arrow Rock which did business until Superintendent of Indian Affairs William Clark ordered him to leave due to the increased hostilities between the white settlers and existing "native" residents. By 1817 the area had a ferry service, operated by Henry Becknell, the brother of Santa Fe Trail Company's William Becknell. The fresh water springs area in Arrow Rock was the first stop from Franklin along the Santa Fe Trail.

The town of Arrow Rock was laid out by 1829. Now on Main Street, antique stores, high quality craft and gift shops intermingle with historic buildings. Borgman's Bed and Breakfast has four rooms to let, all of which have the original wide plank floors. The proprietor says "each large room is furnished with antiques and a handmade quilt used on each bed. Part of this home was built before the Civil War and more rooms were added afterward."

On Main Street's north side, visitors may trod planks the length of the storefronts. For in 1853, the ruling body established by Arrow Rockians wanted dry feet and less dirt and gravel in their stores, so they approved the construction of a boardwalk. Late in 1850, townfolks initiated another improvement; stone gutters (accomplished by slave labor) which still survive. Arrow Rock Country Store sells foods as well as gifts and it also has wonderful children's books and books portraying the region's history.

A widely known attraction in theatre circles is the Lyceum Theatre, where professionals perform repertory theatre during the summer months. Lyceum productions play in a 120-year old Gothic Revival church. Call (816) 837-3231 or 837-3311.

The John P. Sites, Jr. Pioneer Gunshop (1844) contains several of the weapons made during Arrow Rock's early years. Many settlers purchased guns from Sites prior to their journey farther west.

Arrow Rock Tavern (1834) has survived as a tavern, hotel, home, or restaurant since its builder Joseph Hutton first opened its doors. This

The Arrow Rock State Historic Interpretive Center.

A spinning demo during Arrow Rock's craft weekend.

Federal Style structure probably served as a residence initially, then became an inn, and then a general store. A second floor ballroom was added later.

Arrow Rock Tavern functioned as a center for political and social activity. Taverns of that era, it has been written, provided the traveler sleeping space, with two or three sharing a bed, frequently with strangers. In general, tavern food varied from "corn bread and common fixin's for 25 cents" to the elegant seven course meal avec champagne or mit Rhine wine, for $1.00. KATY Trail-ers enjoy "Tavern ambience" in a large dining room. Its General Store is stocked to reflect supplies sold in the 1850's; the weather vane atop the tavern was retrieved from an 1880s steamboat.

Perhaps Dr. John Sappington is Arrow Rock's most famous resident. Sappington advocated the use of quinine to treat malaria; his *Theory and Treatment of Fevers* (1844) was the first medical text printed west of Mississippi River. But George Caleb Bingham also lived in Arrow Rock, in a brick house he built in 1834. He began painting professionally when asked by four Arrow Rocker friends to do their portraits. Bingham's 1834 portrait of the Sappingtons now hangs in Arrow Rock Tavern. He painted the famed "County Election," inspirated (both inspired and pirated) by/from the 1830s Saline County Court House. A thousand people lived in Arrow Rock by 1860. During the Civil War, soldiers burned much of Arrow Rock, and the town "declined" as the Missouri River changed her course and Arrow Rock's river town inheritance vanished. Chicago ain't the only town remembered by or beset by fires. Arrow Rock also knew death by fire, in 1873, and again in 1901. But the Phoenix rises.

Site along the Trail.

In the early 1970s, Hollywood hit Arrow Rock. She became the setting for two movies based on Mark Twain's Tom Sawyer and his wirey chum Huckleberry Finn.

Arrow Rock State Historic Site offers picnic and camping areas (200 acres) and a newly opened visitor center with Boonslick interpretive exhibits: (816) 837-3330.

Events Calendar (816) 837-3470

Friends of Arrow Rock (816) 837-3231

KATY TRAIL
The Proposed Route

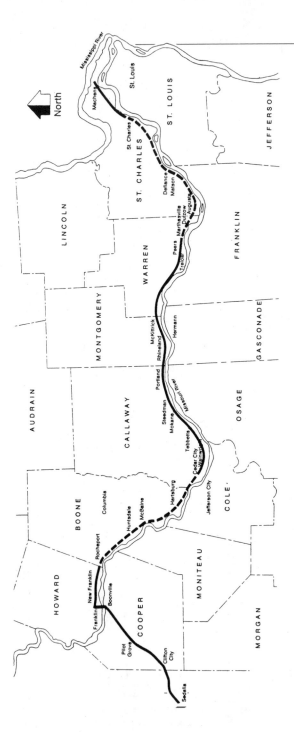

Maps courtesy of Missouri Department of Natural Resources

SOURCES

Our trail guide, naturally, a dissertation it's not. Historical references (except our attempts at spoof-humor) come from the following sources. We elect not to litter or sidewind readers with in-body citations. We ask acceptance of information as documented "somewhere in" these sources. Please write to us re: any goof-ups you think we've made.

A Boone County Album. Sesquicentennial Committee 1971
A Pocket History of the United States, 1976
Bicentennial Boonslick History, 1976
Caldwell, D. G. Russell. Rocheport: River Town
Campbell, M. Museum of Once-Sunken Treasures KC Star 11/3/91
Crighton, J. History of Columbia & Boone County, 1987
Daulton, F. Rails to Trails, Columbia Missourian 5/4/88
DeVoto, B. The Journals of Lewis and Clark, 1978
Dyer, B. Boonville: An Illustrated History, 1987
        and Big Canoe SongbooK, 1991
Garbus, K. One Way to Recycle RR Route, KC Star 8/11/91
Griffith, C. R. The Missouri River 1942
Havig, A. Columbia, 1984
History of Boone County. Ramfre Press, 1882
Krodel, B. Hiking Coast to Coast, USA Today 8/29/91
Larkin, L. Vanguard of Empire, 1961
Levens, H. N. Drake. A History of Cooper County, 1876
Lienhard, H. From St. Louis to Sutter's Fort, 1961
Marshall, H. Now That's a Good Tune, UMC 1989
Masterson, V.V. KATY Railroad & Last Frontier Town, 1981
McCall, E. Conquering the Rivers, 1984
McClure, C.C. History of Missouri, 1920
McLaughlin, T. KATY Trail expands westward, Columbia Daily Tribune 1/6/92
McReynolds, E. Missouri: A History of Crossroads State, 1962
Meyer, D. The Heritage of Missouri, 1963
Missouri's Black Heritage, 1980
Missouri Day by Day, Vol I, 1942
Missouri: Facts and Figures. Div. of Tourism, 1990
Missouri: Its People and Its Progress, 1945
Nagel, P. Missouri, 1977
New Beginnings, Columbia Missourian 2/20/91
Original Journals of Lewis/Clark Expedition, Vols 6-7, 1969
Pause in Missouri: People, Places, and Things,
Phillips, C. Missouri: Mother of the American West, 1988
Pierce, D. Exploring Missouri River Country, DNR
Prouse, M. Arrow Rock: 20th Century Frontier Town, 1981
Rainey, T.C. Pioneer Sketches of Arrow Rock/Vicinity, 1971
Roger, A. Lewis and Clark in Missouri, 1981
Rose. F. Boone's Lick Legends, Col. Daily Tribune 11/29/87

Sanders, M, Future holds new life Weekly Missourian 10/5/88
Satterfield, A.   The Lewis and Clark Trail. 1978
Scheff, R. Vintage Missouri: A Guide to Wineries, 1991
Summerhays, S. Long Road to Hoe. Col. Daily Tribune 12/1/91
      and Trailside Towns try to resurrect, 12/27/91
Sunder, G. In the Footsteps of Lewis and Clark, 1970
Swift, J. Steamboating/Transshipment on Missouri, Fall 1983
The KATY Flyer, Fall 1991
The Missouri Quick-Fact Book, 1991
The WPA Guide to 1930's Missouri, 1986
Tracing Roots in the Missouri River Town, KC to St. Louis,
White, E. A Century of Transportation in Missouri, 1920

Interview w/David Sapp, 1/9/92, and others who should know

TRAIL MILEAGE CHART

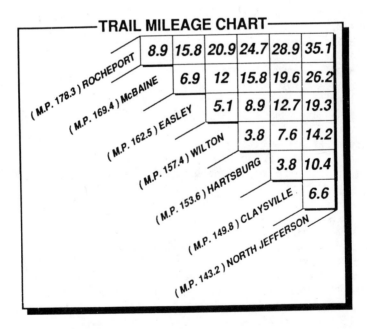

	8.9	15.8	20.9	24.7	28.9	35.1
(M.P. 178.3) ROCHEPORT		6.9	12	15.8	19.6	26.2
(M.P. 169.4) McBAINE			5.1	8.9	12.7	19.3
(M.P. 162.5) EASLEY				3.8	7.6	14.2
(M.P. 157.4) WILTON					3.8	10.4
(M.P. 153.6) HARTSBURG						6.6
(M.P. 149.8) CLAYSVILLE						
(M.P. 143.2) NORTH JEFFERSON						

A Bit of Missouri State Legislative Work

CRINOID (a mineralization of an animal with a plant-like appearance) is the state of Missouri's official fossil.

GALENA (a naturally occuring lead sulfide and ore-bearing mineral of lead) is the official mineral.

MOZARKITE (a form of chert or flint) is Missouri's State Rock.

THE HONEY BEE is the state insect.

EASTERN BLACK WALNUT is the offical nut of Missouri, while the lovely wild dogwood, full of flower in rocky open woods, bluffs, and thickets is the state tree.

The blossom of the common RED HAW, also known as the HAWTHORN, is the official state flower.
The state bird is the native BLUEBIRD.

71 KATY TRAIL

Regularly Scheduled Events Along KATY Trail

February

Jefferson City - Winter Environmental Experience, 1st Sat.   Mid-Missouri Conservation Society (314) 893-4184

March

Boonville - Old Time Fiddlers Contest, 3rd Sat.

April

Arrow Rock - Easter Parade & Egg Hunt (816) 837-3470
Jefferson City - Hometown Heritage Week (314) 635-1171

May

Arrow Rock - Gospel Sing/Federated Church (816) 837-3210
Arrow Rock - Antique Show/Art Festival/Old School House
3rd week, 837-3470
Jefferson City - Mid-MO Conservation Society Meeting/Program
4th Thurs, Conservation Headquarters

June

Arrow Rock - MidAmerica Knife Makers Demo/Old School House
  (816) 263-4639
Arrow Rock to Wellington Covered Wagon Santa Fe Trail Re-enactment, June 21-27, 1992 Lexington (MO) Briddle & Bit Club
Boonville - Heritage Days (816) 882-2721

Missouri Climate

Missouri weather is described as humid continental with long summers and variable weather. We have periods of almost constantly changing weather and periods when weather is settled and stable.

Winters are fairly brisk and stimulating, seldom severe. Average January temperatures vary from 25 to 34 F. Summers are warm and humid; July brings pleasant 70 or breaks into the upper 90s.

Rainfall mostly occurs in the spring and during the May-August crop growing season, but snow on the trail is a wonderous sight.

July

Boonville - County Youth Fair/Fairgrounds (816) 882-5661
Jefferson City - Mid-MO Conservation Society Meeting/Program
 4th Thurs, Conservation Headquarters

August

Boonville - Lazy Day on the Missouri River (816) 882-5858
Boonville - Missouri River Arts Festival (816) 882-7977

September

Arrow Rock - Folk Music Fest/Old School House (816) 882-7821
Boonville - MS Bicycle Ride KC to Boonville (816) 882-2721
Boonville - MO River Valley Steam Engine Show 796-4742
Boonville - Cooper Cty Fair Grounds 1st wk after Labor Day
New Franklin - Santa Fe Trail Days, 3rd Sat/County Hist Soc.

October

Arrow Rock Craft Festival, Old School House (816) 837-3470
Arrow Rock State Historic Site Festival 2nd wkend, 837-3330
Arrow Rock Halloween Storytelling/Old School House 444-5537
Boonville - Festival of Leaves & Porkfest (816) 882-2721
Jefferson City - Mid-MO Conservation Society Meeting/Program
4th Thurs, Conservation Headquarters

Mile Post Markers (MP)

KATY Trail is marked every mile with a sign post that carries the traditional railroad mileage noting system. (FYI: MP 27 is at the eastern end of the rail at Machens and MP 227 is in Sedalia.) To determine the distance you travel, subtract the MP number at the trail point where you begin from the mile post number you reach on the trail.

Emergency 911

County Sheriff Offices

Boone (314) 875-1111
Callaway (314) 642-7291
Cole (314) 634-9160
Cooper (816) 882-2771
Howard (816) 248-2477

Hospitals

Jefferson City

Memorial Community, 1432 Southwest Blvd, (314) 635-6811

Still Regional, 1125 Madison (314) 635-7141

St. Mary, 100 St. Marys Medical Plaza, (314) 635-7641

Columbia

University Hospital, 1 Hospital Dr., (314) 882-4141

Boone Hospital, 1600 E. Broadway, (314) 875-4545

Columbia Regional Hospital, 404 Keene (314) 874-9000

Boonville

Cooper County Memorial, South Hwy B, (816) 882-7461

Supply List

First aid kit
CombSun screen
Rain gear
Sweater/jacket
Serviette
Water bottle & bottle cage
Coins for phone call(s)
Identification
Hat/Helmet
Lederhosen/staff for style
Cyling gloves
Pocket trash bag

Spoke wrench
Presta valve adapter
Tire patch kit
Tire tools
Phillips/straight screwdrivers
Metric Allen wrenches
Metric wrenches

Though KATY's daylight hours only, carry a mini flashlight or equip your bicycle with a headlight, just in case...

KATY TRAIL 74

Trail User's 10 Remindments

KATY Trail is bicycle-patrolled by staff from the Department of Natural Resources (DNR). If you want to obtain a special event permit, or wish to make comment about the trail, call DNR: 1-800-334-6946.

KATY Trail is open year round to the public, daylight hours only. Following are paraphrased rules of DNR.

1. Stay on the trail. Respect state property and do not trespass onto private property through which the trail provides a corridor.

2. Do not climb bluffs.

3. Stay a safe distance from the Missouri River. She is a swift and unforgiving stream whose slippery banks may cause injury, lead to life-threatening accident, other danger.

4. Be alert to obstacles on the trail (fallen rocks, wildlife, washed out pathways, etc.).

5. Pets must be restrained with leashes, for their safety and to keep them off private land.

6. When approaching oncoming trail users, move to the right side of the trail. Use caution when crossing bridges; especially help children to cross.

7. Stop or yield at all road crossings. Trail users must yield at all farm crossings and private drives.

8. Plan safe distances of walking, bicying, hiking, jogging. Do not over exert or over stress your particular physical condition. On long trips, carry water and energy foods.

9. Do not trash the trail. Carry a litter bag which you can empty at trail head points.

10. Cyclists, when passing someone, say "On the left" and/or ring your bike bell. Cyclists also should peddle at slow, safe speeds when crossing over bridges and passing pedestrians, and avoid suddent stops and quick turns on the Trail's loose gravel.

**Division of Parks, Recreation and Historic Preservation
Dept. of Natural Resources: 1-800-334-6946
Missouri Div. of Tourism: (314) 751- 4133**

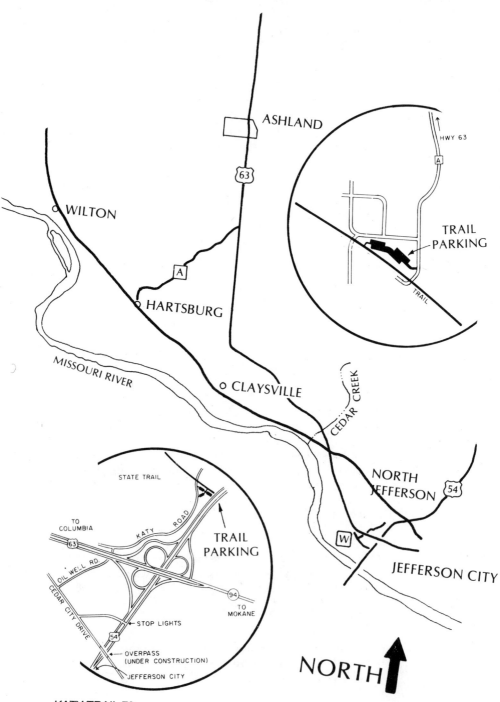

KATY TRAIL 76

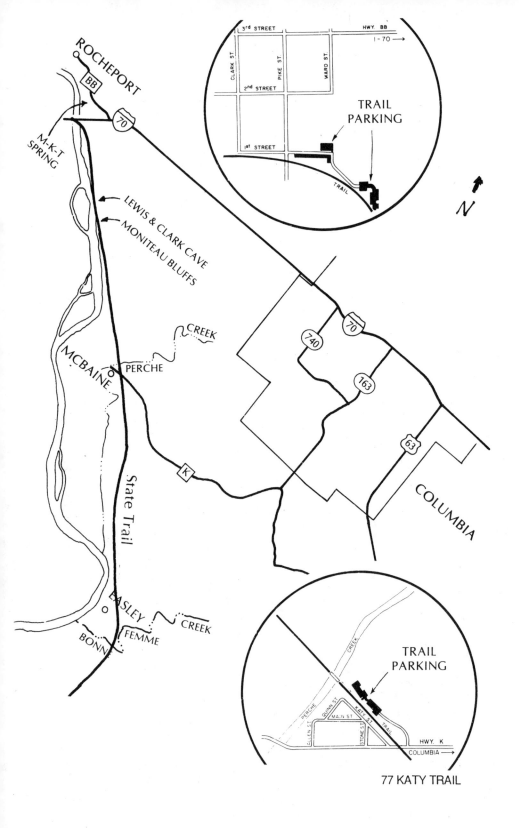

77 KATY TRAIL

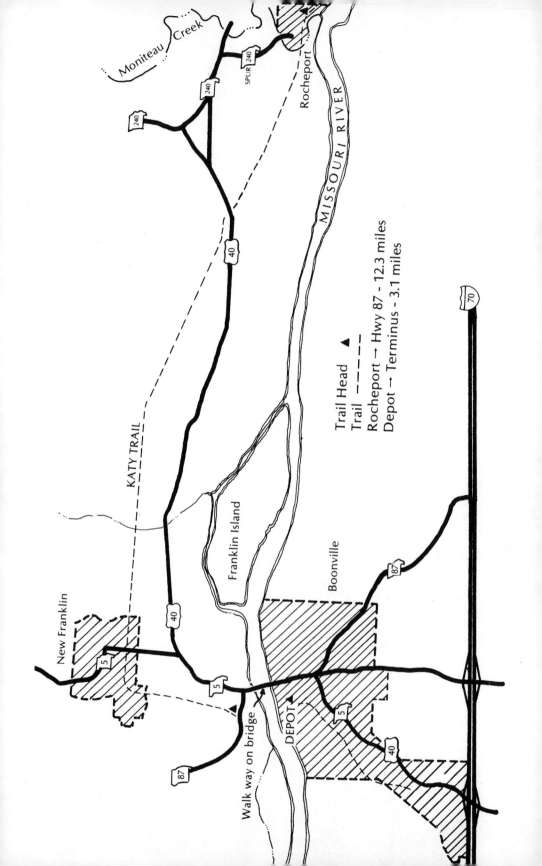

Moniteau Creek

240

SPUR 240

240

Rocheport

MISSOURI RIVER

240

40

KATY TRAIL

Trail Head ▲
Trail - - - - -
Rocheport → Hwy 87 - 12.3 miles
Depot → Terminus - 3.1 miles

70

Franklin Island

Boonville

87

New Franklin

40

5

5

87

5

40

DEPOT

Walk way on bridge

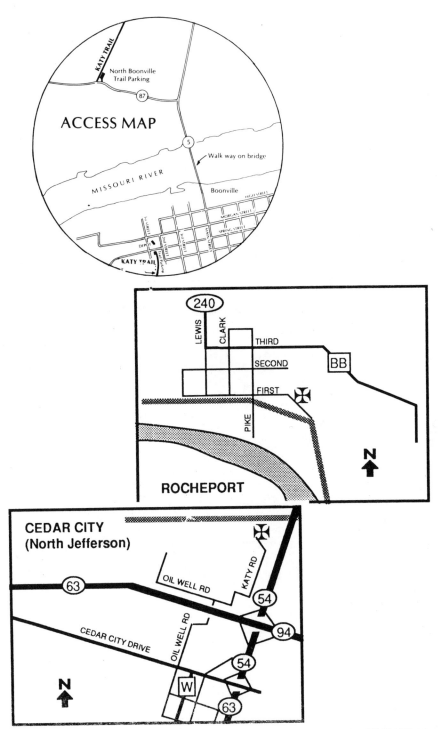

ACCESS MAP

KATY TRAIL

North Boonville
Trail Parking

87

5

Walk way on bridge

MISSOURI RIVER

Boonville

HIGH STREET
MORGAN STREET
SPRING STREET
DEPOT
KATY TRAIL

240

LEWIS
CLARK
THIRD
SECOND
BB
FIRST
PIKE

N

ROCHEPORT

CEDAR CITY
(North Jefferson)

63
OIL WELL RD
KATY RD
54
OIL WELL RD
CEDAR CITY DRIVE
94
54
N
W
63

79 KATY TRAIL

Excerpts from UNION STATION

Copyright 1984 Charles Guenther

Once there was a prairie with scrub oak, an occasional pool
Where buffalo grazed and drank, their rumbling track
Mistaken for thunder shook the morning air,
Flushing out every creature that flies or springs.

And here the Osage camped where the bed of the pool
Lay, settlers came for the pure springs
And the black earth, mountain men left to track
Deer and beaver from where the Missouri ends
Up to its headwaters in the lands of silence,
And boatmen labored and danced to some old French air.

Under cedars and cottonwoods, ghosts in the moonlit air,
Lovers pressed on the grass by the glassy pool
(Where have they gone! Only a winter silence
Lies with the faded stones by the vanished springs).
The valley reclaimed, the pond was drained to the ends
Of its arms and coves to lay the parallel track,

Nineteen miles of tentacular steel track!
Gray stones and Spanish tiles, spires in the air,
Rose over the roundhouse where the landscape ends,
Apex and terminus once of a human pool
That swarmed to the coupled cars with the well-oiled springs
Where rolling stock stands here rusting in silence.

In the lace of a trestle and track, a sunken pool,
Honeysuckle hangs in the air: a new life springs
Until everything ends once more in the music of silence.

"Union Station" appeared in a 1984 photo folio in celebration of the 90th anniversary of St. Louis' Union Station (prior to renovation). Excerpts of this poem reprinted here with permission of Charles Guenther